DAY OF THE DEAD

20 CREATIVE PROJECTS TO MAKE
FOR YOUR PARTY OR CELEBRATION

PAULA PASCUAL
AND REBECCA WOODS
WORDS BY PHILLIP TANG

BARRON'S

First edition for the United States and Canada
published in 2017 by Barron's Educational Series, Inc.

Copyright © Carlton Publishing Group 2017

Craft projects on pages 14, 18, 20, 36, 44, 46,
48, 52, 54, 64, 70, 72, 74 by Paula Pascual.
Recipes on pages 22, 28, 30, 32, 34 by
Rebecca Woods.
Make-up on pages 66, 68 by Nicki Henbry.

All inquiries should be addressed to:
Barron's Educational Series, Inc.
250 Wireless Boulevard
Hauppauge, NY 11788
www.barronseduc.com

ISBN: 978-1-4380-1101-1

Library of Congress Control No.: 2017939978

Printed in China

9 8 7 6 5 4 3 2 1

CONTENTS

INTRODUCTION

The *Día de los Muertos* (Day of the Dead) is an annual Mexican celebration. It is a time of festivities when family and friends gather to remember and commune with the departed. It is believed that the spirits of deceased ancestors and loved ones return to the realm of the living for a short time each year to spend time with their families. UNESCO has declared the festivities around the Day of the Dead an Intangible Cultural Heritage of Humanity.

Unlike some cultures that consider a visit to a cemetery to be a solemn affair, this is not a time of solitary reflection but an occasion of joyous remembrance and merriment. It is shared with the souls of departed loved ones, young and old, human and animal, who return to the world of the living. Altars are set up with offerings to guide and lure the spirits back from the underworld or from heaven.

Day of the Dead celebration in Morelia, Michoacán, Mexico.

HISTORY

These festivities spring from a different tradition than Halloween and can be traced back to ancient Aztec customs. There is evidence that the rituals were handed down from the more ancient Olmecs. So, the Day of the Dead has its roots in pre-Hispanic civilizations starting from more than 3,000 years ago.

Before the Spanish arrived in Mexico, an Aztec custom of communing with the deceased lasted the whole month of what is now August. It was a time of joy, and mourning was forbidden. The spirits already faced a tough journey back from the underworld, and tears would only make the path more slippery and dangerous. It was believed that the soul was eternal and could move freely between worlds.

Left: *A Day of the Dead altar mixes Catholic and pre-Hispanic elements.* Opposite: *Decorated graves, Xochimilco, Mexico.*

In these times, families would often have an ancestral tomb or burial spot close to home or even under the house. The dead were buried there, so it was felt that the departed were not gone but merely continued on in a different plane, but in the same home. The Day of the Dead (or month) allowed communication with these ancestors.

When the Spanish arrived with Catholicism, the tradition of celebrating the dead fit well with the solemn days of All Saints' Day (November 1), a holy day of obligation, and All Souls' Day (November 2). So the two traditions were merged and the Aztec dates altered to match those of the Catholic church. This fusion is reflected today on any Day of the Dead altar, which can contain images of both the Virgin Mary (and her Mexican manifestation, La Virgen de Guadalupe) and skulls and skeletons from Aztec traditions.

Today's festivities take place over two days. The Day of the Dead is on November 2, but the celebrations commence from November 1. Mexicans believe that the returning spirits visit from midnight on October 31 and depart again for the underworld at the end of November 2. In most parts of Mexico, it is believed that the spirits of *angelitos* (deceased babies, infants, and children) or "little angels" arrive at midnight on October 31. They spend the entire day of November 1 with the living and then leave. This day is called *Día de los Inocentes* (Day of the Innocents) or *Día de los Angelitos* (Day of the Little Angels). The spirits of adults are thought to arrive at midnight on November 1, and are

honored on November 2. This is the focus of the Day of the Dead. Originally, these two days were celebrated for 20 days in two separate Aztec months. The first, Miccailhuitontli, honored the spirits of children, and the second, Hueymiccailhuitl, celebrated the return of adults.

Mocking death is a part of Mexican culture. It is reflected in everyday life. It has been popularized in art. It is seen in handicrafts and in children's toys that allow them to act out funerals with miniature coffins and figurines of undertakers. That is not to say they do not mourn the dead or fear death. They simultaneously mourn while celebrating a person's life with happiness.

Making It Your Own

As the Day of the Dead is more of a cultural activity than a religious one, it is possible to integrate it with your own beliefs—just as it was incorporated into Mexican Christianity and continues to evolve. It is an interesting way to celebrate and honor loved ones who have passed on. A Day of the Dead party or event allows you to use a broad range of artistic and culinary creativity to show appreciation for the departed. It is an opportunity for children to understand death and to learn about the lives of family members through fun tales and remembrance. In this spirit, this book provides 20 projects for a Day of the Dead celebration, taking key beliefs and visual elements from the festival as inspiration.

PART 1
RITUALS

DECORATED ALTARS

The construction of *ofrendas* (altar offerings) is an important part of honoring the dearly departed in the lead-up to the Day of the Dead. The altars are usually set up at home, but even those who do not have close family or friends who have passed away can join in the festivities by visiting public buildings and local buildings such as art galleries and restaurants. Schools also regularly create altars with the children that display messages of peace and love as a way to instill a sense of pride about the traditions of Mexico and the pre-Hispanic world. There is a lot of flexibility in the style of altars, since their purpose is to honor specific loved ones. It is not uncommon to find college students and young people creating their own makeshift altars to beloved musicians and artists.

There are popular elements that can be used to make an altar in any arrangement on a table or in a garden. A full altar usually has three levels to represent life: heaven on the top, the earthly plane on the middle level, and the underworld at the base. You can stack crates, small tables, or shelving to build up three levels.

Different items belong to each realm. Religious figures belong on the top level. Food and drink offerings and sugar skulls can be placed on the middle level along with other items of the living, such as photos and personal mementos of the departed. The bottom level represents Mictlán, the Aztec realm of the dead, and figures of skeletons and La Catrina (Lady of the Dead) are good

to place here. Incense, candles, and *papel picado* (paper banners) can be placed on any level.

Looking at the completed altar, you will notice that it is a cultural relic. Mexicans are overwhelmingly mestizo, referring to the mixed ethnicities of Spanish and indigenous. Their mixed culture is reflected everywhere, including in the altars, which combine the ideas of the afterlife as the Catholic heaven with Aztec beliefs about the underworld and the four elements of nature. Water, earth, wind, and fire are represented in the offerings. Water and earth are reflected with food, drinks, and flowers, while wind is represented by the lightweight *papel picado*, and fire by candles.

Opposite: Candlelight guides the spirits to the altar. Right: Elaborate altar decorated with a profusion of marigolds in a courtyard in San Miguel de Allende, Guanajuato, Mexico.

Sugar Skulls and Skeletons

A skull represents the soul of the departed. Traditionally, the name of that person is written on the forehead and the sugar skull is laid out on the *ofrenda* or gravesite. Sugar skulls are happy, bright, and made with colorful icing. Glittering adornments and reflective foil add to the festive look. Skull- and skeleton-shaped toys, puppets, and candy are also used as adornments.

Candles and Incense

Velas (candles) are placed in glass holders around the altar. The glass holders often display images of the Virgin Mary, revealing the Catholic influence of this fusion tradition. The flame is a symbol of hope and faith and the element of fire. It helps to guide the returning spirits from the underworld toward the *ofrenda* for the night. Often a candle is laid out for each remembered soul. The fragrant scent of incense also helps attract the souls of the honored. The incense used is copal, which is made from pine resin. The smoke is a medium to commune with the spirit world.

Marigolds and Sand Tapestries

Another way to signal the path to the living is through the vibrant orange and yellow colors and strong scent of the *cempasúchil* flowers (marigolds). Plants in pots or vases adorn altars and the home. The petals are scattered on the floor around the altar and form a bright path from the street leading all the way through a building to the *ofrenda*. The marigold was the flower of Mictecacihuatl, the Aztec lady of death who was the precursor to La Catrina.

Colorful sand is laid out in tapestries surrounding the more elaborate public altars. The designs can be of traditional Mexican motifs, skulls, and crosses.

Right: *Brightly colored personalized altar dedicated to a loved one.* Opposite: *Sugar skulls (see pages 22–23).*

Photos and Mementos

Altars act as a storyboard of the lives of the deceased. Photos and personal possessions are displayed in their honor. *Ofrendas* in public places, such as museums or even bars, often will honor heroes who have symbolic meaning to their patrons. This can be done through photos of famous people, especially of those who have recently passed away. Religious figures, such as statues of the Virgin Mary and angels, can be placed according to personal beliefs. The construction of *ofrendas* is a cultural tradition, not a religious one, so it is quite flexible.

Salt and Water

A vessel to hold salt and another for water have symbolic value. Salt is purifying and associated with preserving bodies. Water and rain were mysterious and sacred to the Aztecs, but later water also became a symbol of baptism and purification under the Catholic church.

MARIGOLD PAPER POM-POMS

The most popular *flor de muertos* (Day of the Dead flower) is the marigold. Its vibrant color and pungent scent guide the spirits to the altar. It also represents the fragility of life. Make extravagant clusters of these easy marigold pom-poms to display in vases, or to place flat on your table or altar. You can never have too many.

This pom-pom technique is versatile and can be adapted to other projects in this book. The Floral Headdress (page 70) uses the same pom-poms, and these paper flowers can also be incorporated into the Wreath (page 48) or substituted for the flowers that decorate the Mask (page 64). You can even make little ones to use on the Drinking Straws (page 36) to add extra variety to the designs.

How to Make Your Pom-Poms

You can use fewer tissue-paper sheets, but 12 will give you a very dense flower, which reflects the marigold. If you want to increase the size of your flower, increase the number of sheets as well as the length and the width.

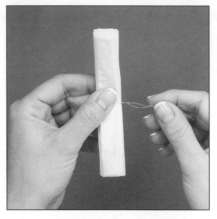

1 Cut 12 sheets of tissue paper that measure 4½ x 8¼ in. (11.5 x 21 cm) and stack them together. Make accordion folds at approximately ½ in. (1.2 cm) intervals.

2 Cut a piece of 28-gauge wire about 2 in. (5 cm) longer than the width of the folded paper. Wrap around the center and twist the ends together at one side.

Materials

Tissue paper in yellow or orange
Florist wire in 28-gauge and
   18-gauge
Chenille stems
Floral tape
Strong scissors
Hot glue gun

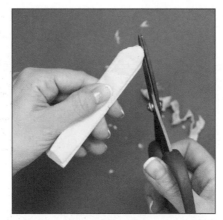

3 Use strong scissors to trim both ends of the tissue to give them a rounded petal shape.

4 Starting from the center, gently separate a single layer of tissue and lift up.

5 Continue to separate the layers, working in a circular manner all around the center, but lifting all layers upward.

6 When there are only about three or four layers left, make cuts into these layers up to ¾ in. (2 cm) to separate the petals.

7 Take two chenille stems and attach to the wire on the pompom using a length of 18-gauge wire to secure.

8 Fix the chenille and wire with a hot glue gun. Finish by wrapping floral tape tightly around the stem.

CANDLE HOLDERS

Candles are an important element of the Day of the Dead, as they guide the spirits to the world of the living. This decorative project is a great way to recycle glass jars of different shapes and sizes using a basic papier-mâché technique with *papel picado* (cut-paper designs). The translucent tissue paper allows candlelight to shine through and enhance the patterns.

How to Make Your Candle Holders

1 Measure the height and circumference of your jar. Cut a piece of white tissue paper to this size.

2 Apply a thin layer of glue to the surface of the jar with a soft brush, and gently roll it along the length of the paper sheet to attach. Leave to dry.

3 Cut a piece of colored tissue paper that is the same height, but slightly longer than the circumference of the jar. Fold in half, lengthwise, then again, and again, until it is about 1 in. (2.5 cm) thick.

4 Draw around one of the templates on page 82, or create your own design; cut out the pattern with scissors. Open up the tissue paper.

5 Apply a thin coat of glue over the white tissue paper, and attach the colored paper in the same way as before, overlapping the ends. Be careful not to tear the tissue.

6 Measure the rim of the jar and cut a strip of tissue paper in a contrasting color. Brush a thin layer of glue around the rim, and gently press the tissue in position.

7 Add a sealing coat of glue over the paper to protect the delicate designs. Repeat with other jars and different colors.

Materials

Glass jars in different sizes
Tissue paper in white and
    a range of bright colors
White glue/craft glue
Scissors
Soft paint brush

SKELETON BOX

Recycle a small box or fruit crate to display this charming dancing skeleton. The box can take a prominent position on your altar, or use it as the centerpiece of your table for a celebration with family and friends.

Materials

Box, at least 7 x 19 in. (18 x 27 cm)
Acrylic paint in yellow, white
Cardstock in white, red, green
Crepe paper in green, white, red, yellow
Coloring markers or colored pencils
Small scissors or craft knife
Paper piercer or large needle
Small paper fasteners or brads
Paintbrush
Measuring tape
Double-sided tape or glue
Eye pin, 1 in. (26 mm)
Pinking shears
Black marker
Jump ring, $\frac{1}{8}$ in. (4 mm) diameter (optional)
Flat-nose pliers (optional)

How to Make Your Skeleton Box

1 Trace or photocopy the skeleton template on page 83 onto white cardstock. Add color to the details, as preferred. Cut out the pieces with small scissors or a craft knife.

2 Pierce the dots at the joint points, including the top of the skull, with a paper piercer or large needle. Construct the skeleton, linking the joints with paper fasteners.

3 Paint the back of the box yellow. Leave to dry.

4 Paint the outer and inner sides of the box white, and leave to dry.

5 Measure the four inner sides of the box frame and cut pieces of red cardstock. Fix in place with double-sided tape or glue.

6 Repeat for the four outer sides of the box with green cardstock.

7 Make a hole in the top of the box about ¼ in. (1 cm) from the front edge with the paper piercer. Feed through the eye pin, and fold the excess on top.

8 To create the roof fringe, trim lengths of the crepe papers to the width of the box and about 1 in. (2.5 cm) deep. Trim one of the long sides with pinking shears and make parallel snips along this side with scissors to create a short fringe. Glue the first strip to the front of the roof so that the fringe overhangs the front edge. Then, glue the next one to overlap the first, and continue with other strips to cover the top of the box. (The photograph on pages 8–9 shows this more clearly.)

9 If the box has quite a deep rim, decorate this edge with a black marker as shown in the photograph on page 20.

10 Open the jump ring and feed it through the hole in the tab on top of the skull and through the eye pin and close, either with flat-nose pliers or just using your fingers. If you don't want to use an eye ring and jump ring, you can use thin wool or string instead.

SUGAR SKULLS

Decorate your skulls with colorful patterns and sparkling jewels. You can make them as plain or elaborate as your skills allow. The skulls pictured here are fairly simple, but see page 13 for more intricate designs. The skulls are for display only: They are not to be eaten. Some skull molds come with a recipe, which you can follow if you prefer.

Ingredients

6 cups (1.2 kg) granulated sugar
3 tbsp (30 g) meringue powder
¾ cup (150 g) powdered royal icing, plus extra for decorating
Food coloring pastes
Plastic gems or sequins

You will also need
Medium-sized sugar skull molds
Spatula
Piping bags and nozzles

Makes 6 medium skulls

How to Make Your Skulls

1 Put the sugar in a large mixing bowl, and add the meringue powder. Add 2 tbsp water. Massage the water into the sugar with your hands until evenly distributed through the sugar. When the mixture is ready (about 5 minutes), the sugar will stick together in a lump and hold an imprint of your fingers when you squeeze a handful.

2 Pack the sugar mix tightly into a mold and press down firmly. Keep adding and pressing to get in as much mixture as possible. Scrape away excess sugar from the back of the mold with a spatula so you have a completely flat surface.

3 Place a tray or plate over the top of the mold, then invert both together to transfer the skull onto the tray or plate. Remove the mold. Repeat until you have used all the mixture—you should be able to make 6 medium-sized skulls, each with a front and a back piece.

4 Leave to set for 4–5 hours. Once they feel firm on top, gently turn them over and leave to dry overnight until completely set.

5 In a bowl, mix the royal icing sugar with enough water to make a spreadable paste. Spread the back pieces of the skulls with a good layer of icing, and press each one onto a front piece. Gently wipe any excess royal icing from around the edge of the seams with your thumb, and leave to dry for at least an hour

until firmly set. You can keep any leftover royal icing for decorating.

6 To decorate, make a thick icing from royal icing sugar and a drizzle of water, and add your chosen color. The icing will need to be quite thick to keep a clean line once piped and not run down the sloped sides of the skull (practice on a sheet of parchment paper first). Transfer the icing to a piping bag.

7 Pipe lines and patterns onto your skull. Change colors and try different piping nozzles to vary the effects. Use the icing to stick on plastic gems or sequins to add a touch of sparkle. Leave the icing to set completely.

22

FOOD AND DRINK

The tradition of laying out food on tombs can be traced back to Aztec times. Food and drink offerings are an important part of any altar as an invitation for the spirits to return and share in the festivities with the living. As the Day of the Dead is a time of joy, food and drink form part of the celebrations so it is important that everything is delicious, indulgent, and beautiful.

People choose dishes and snacks that their loved ones enjoyed eating. Particularly important are meals with strong smells, which are offered up to the deceased to lead the way to our world, and specifically to the altar dedicated to them. Brightly colored food adds to the attraction for the dead (and the living), and orange ingredients, such as sweetened pumpkin, are given pride of place.

In addition to attracting departed loved ones with their favorite foods, the edible offerings have a second, ancient purpose. In Aztec times, the food was given to sustain the deceased on their long journey to the next world. To the Aztecs, the path to Mictlán, the underworld, was a perilous, barren passage, and food was fuel to ferry them across. Today there are some traditional favorites that are used on most *ofrendas* or eaten leading up to the big nights.

Opposite: *Food offerings include* Pan de Muerto *and* mole.

Drinks

The long journey makes the returning souls thirsty, so drinks are required. Chocolate has its origins in Aztec times as an unsweetened, thick drink. It continues to be drunk at Day of the Dead celebrations, but very much in its sweet, milky modern form made from chocolate tablets rather than powder. A similar thick, hot drink is atole. It is blended from the same hominy cornflour used to make tamales, plus cinnamon, anise, and piloncillo, a raw brown sugar. Different variants include flavors such as chocolate, fruit, vanilla, and epazote, a herb used by the Aztecs. Atoles are often sold alongside tamales by street vendors in the morning and evening all through the year, but especially in winter. Fruit juices mixed with water are known as aguas and are part of the festivities as well. Papaya and watermelon are popular.

Right: *Tequila is a popular and traditional drink for the Day of the Dead.*

Tequila and Mescal

Sharing in a graveside alcoholic drink is also a tradition of many celebrations. Mescal, tequila, and pulque are made from the same Mexican plant, the agave. Tequila is the most well-known and commercialized, and is actually a type of mescal, made from only the blue agave plant. Mescal is considered the most artisanal and has a smoky flavor, but in true Mexican fashion, both are a product of the fusion of cultures and were created from distillation techniques brought by the Spanish to the Aztec empire in the sixteenth century. It is enough to use a bottle of tequila or mescal and toast the arrival of the departed with a drink. Before the Spanish, the Aztecs would offer up pulque, a mildly alcoholic fermented drink reserved for spiritual ceremonies.

Mole

There any many kinds of mole—Mexican sauces—but the best known is the black or brown chocolate-based mole poblano. The rich sauce is often cooked with chicken and presented on terracotta plates for the Day of the Dead. Preparing the dish takes plenty of time and attention, making it a praiseworthy centerpiece to any altar. Each type of mole has a complex blend of over 20 spices and ingredients that can include dried fruit, chillies, nuts, and spices such as cinnamon, black pepper, anise, and cumin.

Tamales

Bundles of sticky masa (cornmeal dough) are wrapped in corn husks or banana leaves and steamed. Each has a small filling of endless variations, such as pork and jalapeno or mole chicken, or sweet fillings like pineapple or raisins.

Snacks

Small snacks act as both food and decoration and are a personal choice, but can include fruit (especially oranges, bananas, and loquats for their color), candy, pepitas (pumpkin seeds), and jamoncillo (a caramel fudge that is sometimes colored and shaped like marzipan). Another snack, amaranth, is an ancient grain that the Aztecs used to make decorative skulls, unlike the sugar in modern sugar skulls.

Below: *Tamales.*
Opposite: *A variety of food offerings is left on an altar in Morelia, Michoacán, Mexico.*

PAN DE MUERTO

These delicious sweet buns are traditionally baked to celebrate the Day of the Dead. They are flavored with anise and orange, and the bones on top represent deceased loved ones. Bake them as close to the party as you can for the freshest, softest results. For an extra thick and crispy sugar crust, feel free to add a second layer of sugar glaze once the first one has dried.

Ingredients

4½ oz (130 ml) milk, lukewarm
4½ oz (130 ml) water, lukewarm
2 x ¼ oz (7 g) sachets instant yeast
2¼ cups (575 g) strong white bread flour, plus extra for dusting
⅛ tsp fine salt
½ cup (100 g) caster sugar
5⅔ tbsp (80 g) butter, cubed
2 tsp anise seed, ground
Zest of 2 oranges
2 eggs, beaten
Oil, for greasing

For the glaze
Freshly squeezed juice of 1 orange
5 tbsp (75 g) caster sugar

You will also need
Pastry scraper (optional)
Bone cookie cutter

Makes 16

How to Make Your Sweet Buns

1 Place the milk and water in a measuring cup. Make sure the liquid isn't too hot or it can damage the yeast and prevent it from rising. Sprinkle over the dried yeast, and leave in a warm place for about 10 minutes until the yeast is activated and it starts to bubble on top.

2 Sift the flour into a large bowl, add the salt and sugar, then roughly rub in the butter with your fingertips. Add the ground anise seed and orange zest, then pour in the yeast liquid and beaten egg. Stir until it all comes together into a soft dough.

3 Turn out onto a floured surface and knead for about 10 minutes, until smooth and elastic. The dough will be quite sticky, but persevere and add a little extra dusting flour if needed. A pastry scraper comes in handy for this. Return the dough to a lightly oiled mixing bowl, cover, and leave to proof in a warm place for 1–1½ hours, or until doubled in size.

4 Turn out onto a floured surface and knock it back. Cut off a chunk weighing about 3½ oz (100 g), wrap in plastic wrap, and place in the fridge to slow any further rising. Divide the rest of the dough into 16 even portions, and form into balls. Try to smooth the top surface, tucking the seams underneath to make neat spheres. Place, spaced well apart, on a large, lightly greased cookie sheet. Cover and leave in a warm place to rise for another 30 minutes. Preheat the oven to 350°F/180°C/Gas 4.

5 Remove the dough from the fridge, and roll it out very thinly on a floured surface. Use a bone cookie cutter to stamp out 32 bones.

6 Use a pastry brush to brush the tops of the rolls with a little milk, then crisscross 2 bones on top of each roll. Brush the bones with a little milk, and bake for 16–18 mins, or until risen and golden on top.

7 Meanwhile, put the orange juice in a pan with the sugar. Heat gently for a few minutes until the sugar has melted and the liquid has turned syrupy. Brush the rolls with the glaze when they are fresh out of the oven and still warm.

PUMPKIN AND CHORIZO EMPANADAS

These golden pastries, packed full of spicy Mexican flavors, make a delicious celebratory snack. You can assemble them to the point of filling and keep them in the fridge for a couple of hours, then just pop them in the oven when guests arrive. Chipotle chillies have a wonderful, deep smoky flavor; if you don't want too much heat, simply discard a few of the seeds before you chop them.

Ingredients

Half a small butternut squash, peeled and chopped into $\frac{1}{4}$ in. ($\frac{1}{2}$ cm) cubes (about 1 lb/500 g prepared weight)
4 garlic cloves, unpeeled
3 tbsp olive oil
1 tsp ground cumin
1 tsp ground cinnamon
1 tsp sweet smoked paprika
1 onion, finely chopped
5 oz (150 g) fresh cooking chorizo
3–4 dried chipotle chillies, finely chopped (use a very sharp knife, or blitz them in a spice grinder)
1 tsp dried oregano
2 x 1 lb (500 g) packs shortcrust pastry
1 egg, beaten with 1 tbsp milk, to glaze
Sea salt and freshly ground black pepper
Sour cream, to serve

You will also need
5 in. (12 cm) round cookie cutter

Makes 24

How to Make Your Empanadas

1 Preheat the oven to 400°F/200°C/ Gas 6. Put the squash and garlic cloves in a large roasting pan and drizzle with 2 tbsp of olive oil. Sprinkle over the cumin, cinnamon, paprika, and add a good pinch of sea salt. Mix everything together so the squash is well coated with the oil and spices, and roast for 15–20 minutes, stirring halfway through, until it turns golden and is almost cooked through.

2 Heat the remaining oil in a large frying pan, and add the onion. Cook for 5 minutes or until softened and translucent. Add the chorizo, chipotles, and oregano, and continue to cook for a further 5 minutes or so until the chorizo is fully cooked.

3 Once the squash is cooked, tip the roasted cubes into the chorizo mixture, and stir everything together well. Squeeze the roasted garlic cloves out of their skins and stir into the squash mixture—they should be soft and puréed, but if not, chop them into small pieces with a knife. Season to taste with salt and black pepper, then leave to cool completely. (You can do this in advance, if you like, as it will benefit from a night in the fridge for the flavors to develop.)

4 To make the empanadas, preheat the oven to 375°F/190°C/Gas 5. Roll out the pastry on a lightly floured surface to ⅛ in. (2 mm) thick. Use a 5 in. (12 cm) cookie cutter to stamp out circles from the pastry. Roll out any trimmings to get about 24 circles.

5 Put a couple of heaped teaspoonfuls of the filling on one half of a pastry circle. Brush the egg and milk wash around the edge of the circle, and fold over the other half to enclose the filling in a semicircular shaped parcel. Press the edges together well, then crimp around the edge by pressing with the tines of a fork to seal firmly. Repeat with the remaining pastry rounds to use up all the filling.

6 Brush with egg wash, and bake in the preheated oven for 20–25 minutes until golden brown all over. Serve hot or cold, with sour cream as a dip, if desired.

Vegetarian variation

These are also lovely as a vegetarian snack. Cook the recipe as above, omitting the chorizo. When you come to fill the empanadas, divide the squash mixture evenly between the pastry circles, and top each pile of filling with a little shredded mozzarella—about 1½ tbsp (15 g) per empanada—then continue with the recipe as above. You will need roughly 1½ cups (360 g) of mozzarella.

Ingredients

10 tbsp (150 g) butter, softened
¾ cup (150 g) caster sugar
3 large eggs
1 cup (125 g) self-raising flour
½ tsp baking powder
¼ cup (50 g) desiccated coconut
Zest and juice of 1 large lime

To decorate

5 oz (150 g) white, ready-to-roll
    fondant icing
Black edible markers (you will
    probably need a couple to
    decorate all the skulls)
9 oz (250 g) jet black, ready-to-roll
    fondant icing
Edible glue
2 oz (50 g) red, ready-to-roll fondant
    icing (optional)
Confectioner's sugar, for dusting
    and brushing

You will also need

Skull candy mold or small cookie
    cutter (the skulls need to be
    about 1½ in./4 cm long)
12-cup muffin pan
12 paper cupcake liners
Round cookie cutter the same
    diameter as the tops of your
    cupcakes
Flower plunger cutters (optional)

Makes 12

LIME AND COCONUT CUPCAKES

The sponge for these cupcakes is flavored with Mexican favorites coconut and lime, and the tops are decorated with miniature sugar skulls. Make the sugar skulls days, if not a week, in advance, and decorate them as simply or as intricately as your skills allow. The red flowers add a splash of color, but are optional—the cupcakes still look great without them.

How to Make Your Cupcakes

1 To make the skull decorations: If you are using a mold, dust it with confectioner's sugar. Roll balls of white fondant icing, press into the mold, then turn out and leave to dry. If your mold has less than 12 holes, repeat until you have at least 12 skulls. If you are using a cookie cutter, roll out the fondant icing on surface dusted with confectioner's sugar, and cut out 12 skulls, then leave them to dry for a few hours.

2 Once completely dry, use a black edible marker to decorate the tops with patterns. Take inspiration from the photograph, or search for "sugar skulls" online for ideas. Set aside until needed.

3 To make the cupcakes, preheat the oven to 350°F/180°C/Gas 4 and line a muffin pan with paper liners. Beat the butter and sugar in a large mixing bowl until light and creamy. In a separate bowl, beat together the eggs, and sift the flour and baking powder into a third bowl.

4 Add half the coconut to the creamed butter, followed by half the beaten egg, whisking well between each addition. Repeat with the remaining coconut and egg, then whisk in the lime juice and zest. Fold in the flour.

5 Spoon into the liners and bake for about 15–18 minutes, or until risen and golden. Transfer to a wire rack, and leave to cool completely.

6 Roll out the black fondant icing on a surface lightly dusted with confectioner's sugar. Cut out neat circles with the cookie cutter.

7 Mix a little confectioner's sugar with a drizzle of water to make a quick syrup. Brush the tops of the cupcakes lightly with the syrup, and place a circle of black fondant on each one. Use the edible glue to stick a decorated skull in the center of each black circle.

8 For the flowers, roll out the red fondant icing on a lightly dusted surface. Use the flower plunger cutters to stamp out small blossoms, and adhere them to the top of the cupcakes with edible glue.

LA PALOMA SANGRIENTA (THE BLOODY DOVE)

This is a twist on the classic Mexican cocktail, La Paloma, a combination of tequila and grapefruit. Adding a bit of grenadine gives it a great graduated color effect, and it also adds a little more sweetness to the mix. Serve with a cocktail stirrer to combine all the elements before enjoying.

How to Make Your Cocktail

1 Put the grapefruit juice, tequila, salt, and sugar in a cocktail shaker with ice and shake. Pour into a tall glass (don't strain, you'll want the ice).

2 Drizzle grenadine syrup into the glass, allowing it to sink to the bottom. Top off gently with chilled club soda, pouring it down the side of the glass or over a spoon so that it doesn't disturb the juice too much and you get a pretty graduated effect.

3 Squeeze a lime wedge into the glass, and drop in the empty husk. Stir just before drinking to mix all the layers together.

Non-alcoholic variation
To make a non-alcoholic variation, simply omit the tequila and increase the sugar, to taste.

Ingredients

$3\frac{1}{2}$ oz (100 ml) freshly squeezed grapefruit juice
1 oz (25 ml) reposado tequila (or 2 oz/50 ml to really get the party going)
Pinch of salt
$\frac{1}{4}$ tsp sugar
Ice cubes
Grenadine, to drizzle
Club soda, chilled, to top off
Lime wedge

You will also need
Cocktail shaker
Tall glass
Cocktail stirrer

Makes 1 cocktail

DRINKING STRAW DECORATIONS

Use these delightful floral decorations to brighten up drinking straws for cocktails. Make many variations to use as markers so that your guests never lose their drink.

How to Make Your Drinking Straw Decorations

Materials

Cardstock in hot pink, lime green, purple, yellow, teal
Drinking straws in different colors
Small scissors
Glue or double-sided tape

1 Photocopy or trace the templates on page 84 multiple times onto cardstock of different colors and cut out.

2 Create the banners by wrapping them around the straws and sealing the two ends together with glue or double-sided tape.

3 Using the photograph opposite as a guide, make up lots of flowers by mixing the different templates and gluing each layer together, before attaching to the banners.

PART 2
DECORATIONS

MEXICAN ART AND ARTISANIA

Handmade decorations have a long tradition in Day of the Dead celebrations, and they run parallel with an attempt to respect and hold onto pre-Hispanic culture. The items differ depending on the region, but there are constants.

Papel Picado

These hand-cut pieces of colorful paper are strung out across streets, rooms, and courtyards to give a festive air to most Mexican celebrations. They represent the fragility of life and the element of wind. Stacks of tissue paper are chiselled with intricate designs, which include flowers, angels, birds, words, and historical figures. During the Day of the Dead, skeletons are a popular design, and favorite colors for the *papel picado* are orange, purple, and pink. A skilled crafter can cut through 50 sheets of paper at once. *Papel picado* has existed in some form since pre-Hispanic times. The Aztecs made rough flags of paper from the bark of mulberry and wild fig trees to decorate homes, temples, and the countryside in rituals, often to the god of rain.

Rebozo

The *rebozo* has become an important symbol of Mexican culture. Dating from the 1700s as a head covering for entering temples, today you will still find it draped across the shoulders of women of all classes. The fringed, shawl-like *rebozo* can be woven in simple colors or in an ikat design. It is also sometimes embroidered in brightly colored designs. Mexican artist Frida Kahlo championed traditional Mexican crafts, and was often pictured wearing a *rebozo* as a fashion piece. Indigenous women will use a *rebozo* to carry a baby or food items, to provide warmth, as a sun shield, or even as a childbirth aide. The clothing became associated with rebellion during the Mexican Revolution of 1910. Rebel women wearing the indigenous scarf would hide guns in the folds of the cloth to smuggle through checkpoints set up by the dictatorship. Another important association with the *rebozo* is its use as a death shroud.

Opposite: *La Catrina figurines.*
Below: Papel picado *banner strung across the arch of a courtyard.*

Miniatures

Miniatures of scenes from daily life are placed in small boxes as dioramas. These can be scenes from a barbershop, court case, or a cantina. These highlight how fleeting life is and signify that everybody dies.

Dogs are an image used in figurines. They lead the spirits to their place in the afterlife and back.

Miniatures of the deep orange Monarch butterflies are used. They embody the visiting souls of the beloved. This belief came about because the butterflies make an annual migration to Mexico around November, coinciding with the modern dates of the Day of the Dead.

The Virgin Mary is a popular figure in the form of clay, papier mâché, carved wood, and other materials.

Talavera

The city of Puebla is famous for its ornate talavera pottery, distinguished by its white glaze. The classic color for decorations is blue, though other colors can be used but they must all be natural pigments. The clay is local and natural. It is world-famous and uses techniques that date back to the sixteenth century. In Puebla and across Mexico, talavera decorates the facades of churches and other buildings. Pieces of it can find their way into Day of the Dead celebrations in a tile or a prized food platter. The most common talavera items that are seen on altars are ornate *calacas* (skulls) or statues of La Catrina.

Opposite: Skeleton, with Monarch butterflies and flowers, decorates an altar in San Miguel de Allende, Guanajuato, Mexico.

Clay

While talavera comes from a fusion of Italian and Spanish techniques, and their Arab and Chinese influences further back, the indigenous people of Mesoamerica already had claywork. The earthy material is soon as pots to hold salt, spices, salsas, and snacks on an altar. Orange clear-glazed plates and bowls hold the food offerings and favorite dishes, while clay mugs are used to drink coffee and hot chocolate.

Clay is used to make small statues of an ancient dog, the Xoloitzcuintle. The hairless dog is placed on altars to bring cheer to the spirits of children after their long journey back to the world of the living.

Barro negro (black clay) is a black, smooth claywork from Oaxaca in the south of Mexico. It has a metallic sheen, which is achieved by polishing with quartz before drying is complete. The most well-known item made of *barro negro* is a drinking vessel in the shape of a monkey.

Petate

A *petate* is a woven palm mat that is used in Mexico as a bedroll. In ancient times, and to some in modern times, it could be the bed itself, especially in hot climates for sleeping outdoors. It is rolled up and hung out of the way during the day. The most common place to see it is as a mat to dry out grain, seeds, or tortillas in the sun. As part of an altar, miniature versions of the *petate* are woven to provide a place for the weary returning ancestors to rest once they arrive.

PARTY INVITATIONS

These invitations in the shape of a coffin are decorated with Mexican flower stencils and acrylic paints to give them a slightly distressed look. A final creative touch is provided by the lace embellishments. This is a perfect way to recycle lace fragments passed down through the family, and the handmade finish is a very personal way of announcing your celebration.

How to Make Your Invitations

1 Photocopy the patterned side of the template on page 85 twice onto printable acetate or cardstock.

2 Use a sharp craft knife to cut out the leaves on one copy and the flowers on the other. Cut around the outline to create the stencils.

3 For the invitations, draw around the outer edge of the template onto black cardstock and cut out.

4 Place one of the stencils over the front of the invitation. Gently dab white acrylic paint over the patterns and the edge of the card with a sponge. You need to have an almost paint-dry sponge, so dab excess paint onto a separate piece of cardstock or paper.

5 Repeat the process once the white paint is dry using the other paint colors and new sponges. Lift the stencil and allow to dry.

6 Place the second stencil over the invitation, and repeat the white coat. Leave to dry, then add the color on top.

7 When completely dry, trim off elements of lace and attach to the flower centers with glue. Score the fold line on the reverse of the card with a ruler and the back of the craft knife, and fold in half.

8 If you wish to add an insert, use the inner lines of the template to cut a piece to size, fold and attach along the inside crease of the card.

Materials

Printable acetate or thin cardstock
Black cardstock
Acrylic paint in white, yellow, orange, red, light and dark green
Makeup sponges
White lace
Craft knife and craft mat
White glue
White paper, for inserts

Variation
If you want to make invitations with white card, either omit the white coat or use black to distress the edges of the cardstock.

PAPEL PICADO

Artists traditionally use a hammer and chisel to punch designs into stacks of layered tissue paper, but these designs can be cut out with scissors and a craft knife. Make them using vibrant colors to string across rooms and hallways or to decorate an outdoor area.

How to Make Your Paper Banners

1 Trace or photocopy the templates on pages 86–87 and trim around the outside edges.

2 Cut about 8–10 pieces of tissue paper in a variety of colors to a size slightly larger than the templates, and stack them up.

3 Place the stack on top of one of the templates with the design facing down. Fold the whole stack in half so that you can see the design.

4 Cut out the shapes of the template with scissors or a craft knife, including the outside edge.

Do this carefully to avoid tearing the delicate tissue paper. Repeat with the second template.

5 Separate the layers of tissue and lay them flat, alternating the designs. Make up lengths of your choice using cord, twine, or ribbon. Roll the top edge of the tissue flags around the cord, and attach with small pieces of double-sided tape or dabs of glue. If using glue, be careful because too much will make the tissue paper more fragile when wet.

6 Repeat Step 2 as many times as required to create the number of flags you need.

Materials

Tissue paper in different colors, such as orange, yellow, hot pink, teal, purple, lime green
Cord, twine, or ribbon
Scissors or craft knife
Double-sided tape, white glue, or hot glue gun

WREATH

There are three different types of flowers that make up this exuberant wreath, along with leaves, buds, and berries. Although it will take time to assemble all the elements, the flowers are easy to make, and they will be well worth the effort.

Materials

Thick crepe paper in green, black, purple, hot pink, fuchsia, orange, yellow
Tissue paper in light green, purple, pink, orange, yellow
¾ in. (2 cm) styrofoam balls
¼ in. (1 cm) styrofoam balls
Floral wire, 26-gauge
Green wax-coated floral tape
Cardboard, foamboard, or poster board
Green ribbon, approx. 10 ft (3 m)
Strong scissors
Pinking shears
Hot glue gun and glue sticks
White glue
Small plastic skulls (optional)

How to Make Your Wreath

Gerberas

1 For a small gerbera, cut a strip of green or black crepe paper ⅜ x 8 in. (1 x 20 cm) for the center. Roll it up, and glue down the end.

2 Cut a strip of yellow crepe paper 1 x 6 in. (2.5 x 15 cm) for the outer center. Trim one of the long edges with pinking shears. Make snips with scissors along this edge ⅜ in. (1 cm) deep and ⅛ in. (3 mm) apart. Attach one end to the center and continue rolling. Secure the end as before.

3 Repeat Step 2 for the petals with a strip of purple or pink crepe paper 1½ x 16 in. (3.5 x 40 cm). Make the parallel cuts ¼ in. (5 mm) apart. Open out the petals.

4 To make the sepal or base, trim a piece of green crepe paper about 1 x 3¼ in. (2.5 x 8 cm). Fold along the length several times, cut a V-shape in the top, unfold, and attach around the base of the flower, trimming off any excess.

5 For a medium gerbera, repeat Steps 1–4, with the strip for the petals being 1½ x 16 in. (4 x 40 cm)

6 For a large gerbera, repeat Steps 1–4, but add in a second layer of petals 2 x 16 in. (5 x 40 cm) with the snips ¼ in. (5 mm) apart. Attach this larger strip in the same way, and open out the petals.

For the fringing technique, see also pages 72–73.

Marigolds

1 For a small marigold, cut a strip of orange or yellow crepe paper 1½ x 14 in. (3.5 x 35 cm). Trim one of the long edges with pinking shears. Make snips along this edge about ⅜ in. (1 cm) deep and ¼ in. (5 mm) apart. Roll up the strip and secure the end. Open out the petals.

2 For the sepal see Gerberas Step 4.

3 For a large marigold, repeat Steps 1 and 2 but cut a strip for the flower 2 x 31 in. (5 x 80 cm).

Ranunculus

1 For a small ranunculus, take a small styrofoam ball and cover it in tissue paper using white glue.

2 Transfer the templates on page 89 to crepe paper in a contrasting color and cut out 4 tiny and 12 small petals, making sure that the lines of the crepe paper are vertical in relation to the templates.

3 Overlap the cut in the base of the petals and glue down to give the petals a rounded look.

4 Glue each petal to the ball at the base, starting with the tiny petals and ending with the small petals, overlapping each one.

5 For the sepal, see Gerberas Step 4.

6 For the large ranunculus, repeat Steps 1–5 with the larger styrofoam ball and 4 small, 7 medium, 4 large, and 6 extra large petals.

Buds and Berries

1 For the buds, attach a length of floral wire to the bottom of a large styrofoam ball. Cover it in tissue paper as close in color to your choice of crepe paper.

2 Cut two small ranunculus petals from crepe paper. Glue to the ball, making sure there is plenty of excess at the top.

3 Using the leaf templates on page 89, cut 3 small leaves and attach around the bud. Cover the wire with floral tape and add a few more leaves.

4. For the berries, attach a length of floral wire to the bottom of 3 small styrofoam balls. Cover each in light green tissue paper. Join the wires together and cover with floral tape, then add some crepe leaves.

Leaves

1 Copy the leaf templates, and cut out. Place on green crepe paper with the stretch lines of the crepe at a 45-degree angle on the right-hand side and cut out.

2 Cut the crepe leaves in half from top to bottom, and flip the left half so that the "veins" mirror each other. Overlap the two halves slightly and glue down. Cut a length of floral wire and attach to the back with glue.

To Assemble

1 Enlarge the wreath base template to measure 11½ in. (29 cm) in diameter between the edge of the outer circle. Transfer to cardboard, greyboard, or mountboard and cut out.

2 Secure the end of the green ribbon to the base with a hot glue gun, and wind it around the board to cover it completely. Glue the end at the back.

3 Arrange the larger flowers and secure with the hot glue gun. Continue with the smaller flowers, ending with the buds, berries, and leaves. Add plastic skulls as preferred.

FLORAL FAIRY LIGHTS

Fairy lights are strung up in private and public spaces during the Day of the Dead. Embellish a plain set of lights with paper flowers and *calavera* (skull) designs for your own celebration.

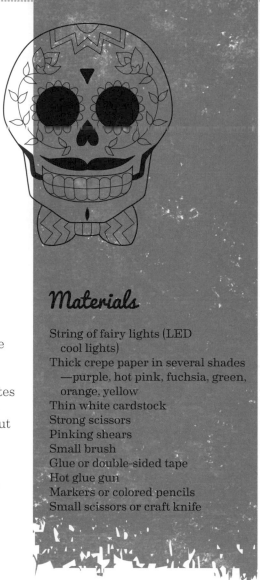

How to Make Your Paper Flowers

1 For each flower, cut a strip of crepe paper measuring 1½ x 18 in. (4 x 45 cm). Trim one of the long edges with pinking shears. Make snips into this edge with scissors about ¾ in. (2 cm) deep and ¼ in. (5 mm) apart. Depending on the strength of your scissors, you can fold the strip and cut into several layers at once.

2 Take a small brush (or any small cylindrical long tool) about the same width as the light fitting and roll the strip around the brush handle. Don't roll up too tightly. Secure the end down with glue.

3 When dry, gently ease the flower off the brush and over one of the lights. Use a hot glue gun to secure the base to the light fitting. Ruffle the petals to separate them.

4 Photocopy the *calavera* templates on page 90 onto white cardstock and add color as preferred. Cut out each one with small scissors or a craft knife.

5 Attach the *calaveras* at regular intervals between the lights by wrapping the tabs at the top of the templates around the cable and securing with a dab of glue or double-sided tape. It's best to do this once the lights are strung up so you can space them for maximum impact.

For the fringing technique, see also pages 72–73.

Materials

String of fairy lights (LED cool lights)
Thick crepe paper in several shades —purple, hot pink, fuchsia, green, orange, yellow
Thin white cardstock
Strong scissors
Pinking shears
Small brush
Glue or double-sided tape
Hot glue gun
Markers or colored pencils
Small scissors or craft knife

TABLECLOTH STENCIL

Use this cut-paper design as a stencil to decorate a plain white tablecloth for your altar or to set out your food and drink on the table at your party. The stencil can also be cut out of colored cardstock to make doilies and tablemats, which are also shown in the photographs opposite and below.

Materials

Tablecloth
Acrylic spray paint or fabric spray
     paint in pink, orange, purple, teal
Cardstock
Colored cardstock (optional)
Masking tape
Craft knife and craft mat

How to Stencil Your Tablecloth

1 Photocopy the template on page 91 at 125% several times.

2 Cut out the design with a craft knife, but do not cut around the outer edge.

3 Starting in one corner of the tablecloth and using a different template for each color, secure the template down with masking tape, and spray over the stencil with acrylic or fabric spray paint. If you want the tablecloth to be washable, use fabric spray paint.

4 To make the doily, photocopy the template onto colored cardstock and cut out the design with a craft knife, including the outer edge.

PART 3
COSTUME

LA CATRINA

La Catrina is the evolution of the "Lady of the Dead" Mictecacihuatl, who was celebrated in ancient Aztec festivals. When the Spanish arrived in Mexico, the worshipping of this death figure became fused with Christian traditions, and evolved into the Day of the Dead. The distinctive image of La Catrina in her Sunday best that Mexicans recognize today didn't exist until subversive illustrator Jose Guadalupe Posada reinterpreted Mictecacihuatl. He engraved the image of a typical madam from French high society in her wide-brimmed hat, but with one big difference—he made her a skeleton, an image of death, to draw attention to the fact that everybody succumbs to death, even the wealthy.

At the turn of the twentieth century, there was a great divide between rich and poor in Mexican society. Mexico was ruled by dictator Porfirio Díaz who opened the door (and control) to capitalists from the U.S. and Europe. Posada's image of La Catrina was a humorous jab at the rich elite who the dictator promoted. He also wanted to give a voice to the folk beliefs of the poor, and the Aztecs who traditionally had worshipped death. Posada made etchings of her, and they were printed on free political broadsides (single-page flyers) and cheap chapbooks aimed at the largely illiterate Mexican lower classes. The wealthy were living it up while the poor suffered, and La Catrina was a parody of these newly rich people.

Posada was a prolific social commentator, and the image of "La Calavera Catrina" became popular from 1910 in the lead up to the Mexican Revolution that would eventually remove the dictator Díaz. The full-length image of La Catrina that we know today became linked to the Day of the Dead when she was painted by Mexican muralist Diego Rivera. He depicted himself and his wife, the artist Frida Kahlo, standing alongside La Catrina in the 1947 mural *Sueño de una Tarde Dominical en la Alameda Central*. Again, La Catrina was used as an image of the complacency of the wealthy in Mexico. From the moment Posada created the image of La Catrina, she has been a smiling figure. This set the tone for the Day of the Dead skeleton imagery to follow, which has always been playful, humorous, and joyous rather than morbid or serious. This ability to laugh at death is a Mexican quality that is personified in La Catrina.

COSTUMES

People young and old in Mexico dress up for the Day of the Dead: women as La Catrina or traditional dress, and men in a suit reflecting El Catrín or a mariachi style. This is often done with skull make-up for both. It is far from the majority who don a costume, but there has been a revival of this tradition in recent years among young people, as Day of the Dead celebrations blur with Halloween.

Women

La Catrina is also known as the "dapper skeleton," and this elegance is shown in the clothes that are worn. The hat should be extravagantly large and wide-brimmed, in black or the same color as the dress. A lace fringe can be added to the hat, but the most important aspect is for it to be adorned with ostrich-style feathers or large flowers, such as fresh or synthetic marigolds or open roses. The hat can be omitted for a headband of flowers. A long feather boa is another important aspect of the costume. Some people reference a funeral by carrying a bouquet of marigolds, roses, or lilies.

The dress is a gown with ample lace, ruching, and visible corsetry that cinches at the waist. This style can have a greater reference to Mexico by using fabric in traditional artisanal styles that incorporate embroidery. The color palette for the dress, flowers, and feathers usually incorporates dark or red-based colors such as purple, maroon, and orange. White dresses are also common for the color associations with death.

The "French" style La Catrina dress can be omitted for a China Poblana style. This is a dress from Puebla, an hour outside of Mexico City, that has come to represent the most classic "traditional" Mexican dress for a woman. Mexican artist Frida Kahlo most famously popularized the China Poblana style of dress. It consists of a white, fringed blouse embroidered with colorful flowers or animals, such as coyotes. The blouse is low cut and can be revealing, which was controversial at the peak of its popularity. The skirt is full and decorated with sequins, while a white slip is worn underneath and is just long enough to peek out at the bottom. A shawl-like *rebozo* is usually worn with the China Poblana outfit.

Men

For men, the traditional look revolves around an elegant suit worn by El Catrín. The dapper gentleman figure is from Mexico's *lotería*. The "lottery" is a bingo-like game with 54 set images. El Catrín is the "dandy," dressed in a bow tie and reminiscent of a circus ringleader.

This look can incorporate funerary elements such as a cutaway coat, white dress shirt, top hat, and handleless walking cane. A red cummerbund is an option, worn with trousers with a line of side piping or pinstripe trousers.

Previous pages and opposite:
Interpretations of La Catrina.

It is common to wear elements of the clothing worn by mariachis—traditional Mexican ensemble street musicians. The clothing is a take on the charro, a classic Mexican horseman similar to a "cowboy" but of a different tradition. A short black rodeo jacket and tight trousers are embroidered with silver edging and adorned with silver buttons. Other elements are the oversized, loose bow tie, heeled boots, and large adorned sombrero. If you are concerned about causing offense or creating a parody of traditional dress, omitting the comically large hat can help.

Women can also be mariachis and have a similar outfit but with a matching stiff, A-line embroidered skirt.

Makeup and Accessories

The makeup for both men and women is the *calavera* (skull). A white base is painted on the whole face, even the lips. Black lines and contouring give the appearance of a skeleton skull. The tip of the nose is painted in, and the lips are drawn over with "teeth." It does not need to be frightening and can be dressed up with colors in swirling patterns. Jewels can be glued along the lines, and the shape of the eye sockets can be colored in. Small crosses, hearts, and flowers can be drawn on the forehead or cheeks to symbolize the familial love aspect of the Day of the Dead.

The devout will wear crosses and rosaries. In some parts of Mexico participants attach shells to their clothes in the belief that when they dance, the noise will rouse the dead.

Masks

Skull masks are used instead of, or in addition to, face painting. The *calacas* (skull masks) have the same designs as the makeup versions, usually in black and white. Some are carved simply out of wood and worn by men. The recent tradition of painting the face as a skull arose out of a blend of cultures in Mexico's history. Skull and devil masks can be found in the traditional crafts of different regions of Mexico. Further back, the Aztecs carved masks out of jade and obsidian for spiritual ceremonies, sometimes as death masks made from the human skulls of slaughtered warriors.

Children

Children are dressed in smaller versions of adult clothing. Increasingly, children are wearing costumes that are more similar to the Halloween tradition. The difference is that children are traditionally in costume for Halloween to disguise them from evil spirits, while the Day of the Dead welcomes the spirits with open arms because they are family members.

Opposite: *The mariachi style.* Left: *China Poblana and El Catrín style.*

MASK

Personalize the mask template by adding your own choice of colors to the design, or photocopy it onto brightly colored cardstock. The top of the mask is embellished with a floral headband in the style of La Catrina, but these can be omitted for a simple skull.

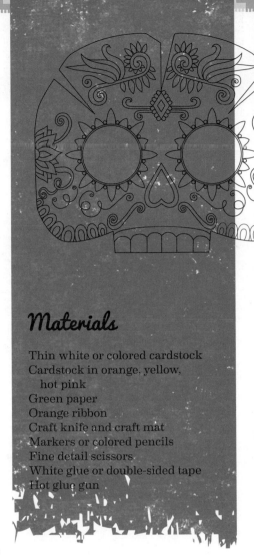

How to Make Your Mask

1 Photocopy the mask template on page 92 onto thin white or colored cardstock. Cut out the eye sockets with a craft knife, and then cut around the outline. Add color to the details, as preferred.

2 Fix the tabs with glue or double-sided tape to add shape to the mask. Attach lengths of ribbon at either side to tie around your head.

3 Photocopy the flower template on page 93 onto yellow cardstock (at 120%), orange cardstock (120%), and pink cardstock (100%) and cut out with scissors.

4 Roll up each flower from the outside edge into the center, and use the hot glue gun to seal the end down at the flower base.

5 From the green paper, cut two pieces 4 x 6 in. (10 x 15 cm) and one piece 6 x 8¼ in. (15 x 21 cm).

6 Take one piece and fold in half. With the crease at the top, cut from the bottom-right corner to the top left. Open it out, and you should have a triangle with a fold in the middle.

7 Start making pleats from one corner into the center, and continue past the fold to the other corner. Glue the bottom corners together and once dry, pull out the pleats a little to shape the leaf. Repeat for the other leaves.

8 Attach the leaves and flowers to the mask with the hot glue gun in an arrangement of your choice.

Materials

Thin white or colored cardstock
Cardstock in orange, yellow, hot pink
Green paper
Orange ribbon
Craft knife and craft mat
Markers or colored pencils
Fine detail scissors
White glue or double-sided tape
Hot glue gun

FEMALE FACIAL ART

Day of the Dead makeup centers on skull imagery.
The eye sockets, nose, and cheekbones are emphasized and
lips are painted with teeth drawn in. Beautiful details are
added in the form of heart and petal designs, curls, and swirls.
For women, the look can be further enhanced with jewels
and gems that pick out the patterns around the eyes
and on the forehead, and the chin.

Makeup items

Nude eyeliner or lip pencil
Bright eyeshadow
Hair gel or wax (optional)
Dark eyeshadow
Black mascara
Black eyeliner
White and red face paint
Black face paint or liquid eyeliner
Flat-back gemstones
Eyelash glue
Makeup sponges and brushes

How to Create the Look

1 Draw the outline for the eye sockets with the nude eyeliner or pencil, going above the brows and following the line of the eye socket. Draw the outline for the nose, creating a V-shape just below the bridge, across the nostrils, and just over the tip. Draw petals on the chin.

2 Use a bright eyeshadow to fill in the whole eye socket area, working the powder into the brows (unruly brows can be smoothed down with a little hair gel or wax). Then use a very dark eyeshadow around the eyes for a smoky look, and apply plenty of black mascara and eyeliner.

3 Cover the rest of the face, including the lips, in white face paint, except the nose and chin petals. Don't extend the white down the neck, but make a clean line around the jawline and just under the chin.

4 Use a small rounded brush and some red face paint to draw little petals around the eye sockets.

5 Fill in the chin petals with red face paint and the nose with black face paint or liquid eyeliner.

6 Using a very fine brush and the black face paint or liquid eyeliner, paint on the forehead design, then outline the eye sockets, little petals, and the chin petals. Next, draw a line from the edges of the mouth out to the hairline, following the shape of the cheekbones, and add some swirls to the cheeks. Draw in vertical lines for the teeth, starting in the middle of the lips and working outward.

7 Stick a gemstone to each petal around the eye sockets with eyelash glue (and anywhere else on the face you want to highlight). Finish by using the dark eyeshadow to shade under the cheekbones, under the chin, and along the jawline.

MALE FACIAL ART

Makeup for men can be kept strong and dramatic with black details drawn onto a white base. Use spiderweb and moustache designs rather than the more feminine symbols of hearts and flowers.

How to Create the Look

1 Draw the outline for the eye sockets, nose, and moustache with a nude pencil. The nose should make a V-shape below the bridge and should not go right out to the edge of the nostrils (see also the photograph on page 74). The eye sockets should come above the brows and follow the line of the eye socket.

2 Cover the whole face and lips in white face paint, except the eye sockets, nose, and moustache. Don't blend the white down the neck, but make a clean line around the jawline and just under the chin.

3 Using a fine brush and black face paint or liquid eyeliner, paint a spiderweb design on the forehead. Paint a line from the edges of the mouth to the hairline, following the shape of the cheekbones. Add swirls and simple petals to the cheeks and chin. Draw in vertical lines for the teeth, starting in the middle of the lips and working outward. Fill in the eye sockets, nose, and moustache.

4 Finally, use dark gray eyeshadow to shade the cheekbones, under the jawline, chin, and any bare skin around the hairline.

Makeup items

Nude eyeliner or lip pencil
White face paint
Black face paint or liquid eyeliner
Dark gray eyeshadow
Makeup sponges and brushes

FLORAL HEADDRESS

Made up of large flower heads, this is a popular modern twist on the La Catrina figure, who is traditionally depicted in a large-brimmed hat. The headdress can be further embellished with feathers and lace, and it can be made as extravagant or as simple as you wish.

How to Make Your Headdress

1 If the headband is covered in ribbon or fabric, sew the black lace to the top of it with a simple running stitch. If it is plastic, use a hot glue gun. You can either wrap it around and leave lengths hanging at either side, or, for wider lace, create a little veil at front or back, as shown in the photograph.

2 Follow Steps 1–4 on pages 16–17 to make up 7 or 8 paper pom-poms in yellow, orange, and red. Use 10 sheets of tissue paper that measure 4 x 8 in. (10 x 20 cm) for each pom-pom.

3 Gently separate all the layers of tissue paper on each pom-pom and lift them upward. Trim the last two or three layers to create more defined petals. Cut the excess wire.

4 Attach the pom-poms to the headband with the hot glue gun, alternating the colors.

Variation
You could also create this headband using some of the flower designs from the Wreath project (see pages 48–51).

Materials

Headband
Black lace
Tissue paper in yellow, orange, red
Floral wire in 28-gauge
Hot glue gun
Needle and thread

FELT HAT DECORATION

This is a simple and effective embellishment for a male costume. Drawing on the funerary style of hat, strips of felt are cut and rolled to mimic the tight petal arrangement of the marigold flower and attached to the brim. Further decoration can be added in the form of feathers and small skulls.

Materials

Felt sheets in red, orange, yellow
Black top hat
Lace ribbon
Scissors
Pinking shears
Hot glue gun
Needle and thread (optional)
Plastic skull
Feathers

How to Make Your Felt Hat Decoration

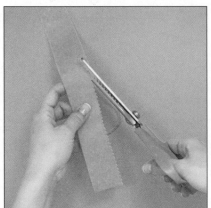

1 Trim strips of felt 1 in. (2.5 cm) wide for the smaller flower head (red), 1½ in. (4 cm) wide for the medium flower (orange), and 2½ in. (6 cm) wide for the large flower (yellow). Use pinking shears along one long side to create a zig-zag edge.

2 Use scissors to make cuts in from the zig-zag edge to about ⅜ in. (1 cm) from the opposite edge. Start with the cuts closer together and then space them farther and farther apart so that the "petals" will increase in size toward the outside of the flower head.

3 Roll up the felt strip starting at the end that has the petals cut closer together.

4 Secure the outside edge with a hot glue gun or use a needle and thread.

5 Cut a small disk of felt to cover the end and fix in place with the hot glue gun. Once dry, fluff out the petals.

6 Cut a strip of lace ribbon to the length of your choice and attach to the base of the top hat with the hot glue gun. Use small amounts each time so it doesn't show through the lace.

7 Attach the flowers, plastic skull, and feathers to the brim of the hat with the hot glue gun in a grouping of your choice. Leave to dry thoroughly.

ROSE CHOKER

The techniques in this project can be used to create chokers and wristbands. For a wristband, it might be best to have a few roses, as shown in the photograph on page 75. For the choker, you could try a whole row of black or red satin roses for a really dramatic effect. Organza is slightly easier to manipulate if you are new to this technique and want to build up your skills.

as shown in the photograph on page 75.

Materials

Black lace
Assorted ribbon:
    red satin 1 in. (25 mm) wide
    red organza 1 in. (25 mm) wide
    black satin 2 in. (50 mm) wide
Choker jewelry findings or
    length of thin black ribbon
Scissors
Needle and black thread
Flat-nose pliers
Needle-nose pliers
Anti-fraying liquid or
    seam sealant

How to Make Your Choker

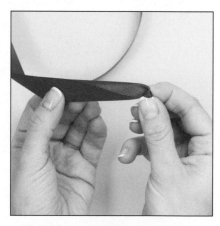

1 Measure your neck and cut a length of lace a little longer. Make a small double fold at each end, and secure with needle and black thread. Place a choker finding with the lace in between the teeth at each end, and flatten with flat-nose pliers.

2 Use needle-nose pliers to attach the chain and closure. To make the red rose, unravel a length of red satin ribbon. Fold the right end lengthwise across the diagonal.

3 Holding tight, start twisting the ribbon from the right edge until you reach the inner corner of the fold.

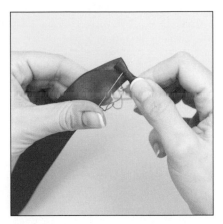

4 Secure tightly with needle and red thread.

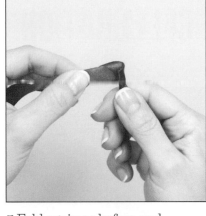

5 Fold again as before and continue to twist the ribbon in from the right-hand side. When reaching the next inner corner, secure it with a couple of stitches, and continue repeating the process.

6 Once you have reached the size of flower you want, secure it well with a few stitches and trim the excess. Some satin ribbons fray a lot, so you can use an anti-fraying liquid or seam sealant. When you trim the ribbon, cut it at a 45-degree angle, and apply a small amount of the anti-fraying liquid. Dab with a cotton swab, and swirl the tip against a paper towel to remove excess liquid.

7 Trim the bottom of the rose so that it's easier to attach to the choker.

8 Repeat with the black ribbon and red organza to create different sizes and textures of flower. Attach to the choker with a few strong stitches.

Variation
As an alternative to using jewelry findings, you can sew a short length of black ribbon at each end to tie the choker in place around the neck.

CELEBRATION

There are a variety of activities that take place around the Day of the Dead that vary by region. Some are standard and are as important as the visual elements.

Cemeteries

In pre-Hispanic times, family members were buried in, or near, the family home. There was no need for a separate home altar. Now that they are in different locations, a visit to the cemetery of deceased loved ones is customary. Often children will lead processions and carry bouquets of marigolds to guide the spirits. Participants bring toys and candy for children who have passed and alcohol for adults.

Once at the cemetery, graves are cleaned and decorated. Village paths are strewn with petals leading from the home to the cemetery to allow the returned to find their way. As the souls return at midnight, in some regions people will celebrate the whole night at the graveside. This vigil involves eating, drinking, and talking until dawn. People can prepare blankets and pillows at home so that the returned can rest after their long crossing.

Poetry and Jokes

Whether at the cemetery or at a home altar, family and friends will join in and recount stories about the deceased. They read *calaveras*, which literally means "skulls" but are short satirical epitaphs of the deceased. It is as if they are in the space and celebrating alongside them. These poetic *calaveras* fondly mock the habits, idiosyncrasies, and personality of the individual. People will tell anecdotes and remind others of funny memories. Prayers are also common for the religious.

People will openly laugh at death in between stories of the honored. There are many tongue-in-cheek euphemisms for death—most of them female—such as *la pelona* (bald lady), *la calaca* (skeleton lady), *la huesada* (bony lady), and *la flaca* (skinny woman). Participants will sprinkle in popular sayings and jokes about life and death, which are customary during the Day of the Dead. For example "*A mí la muerte me pela los dientes*" literally means "Death peels my teeth" or "Death can't touch me." Or "*La muerte es flaca y no puede conmigo*" means "Death is skinny and can't come for me."

As with La Catrina, the *calaveras* have revolutionary roots. They can be traced back to the eighteenth century as a way to parody famous personalities and politicians. These were given alongside illustrated caricatures of the victim in skull form, thus the name *calaveras*. They are linked to Posada, the creator of the La Catrina illustration, who was a great writer of *calaveras*. This style of mockery and illustration is still present in newspapers that poke fun at current famous figures.

For parents, this is a chance to share stories about ancestors that children may never have met or known. Everything is fair game, retelling embarrassing stories as family legends. It is a way to share an oral family history and promote a sense of belonging.

Music and Gatherings

People play music and dance in honor of the returning souls. Live regional music is played in public squares, which are resplendent with *papel picado* and marigold flowers. Skull and devil masks are part of public dances, performances, and processions. In some areas, traditional Aztec dances are held with rhythmic drumming.

Those without a home altar will visit special night openings of museums, galleries, and government buildings to enjoy Day of the Dead altars. There is an element of competition between public buildings to build the most impressive altar. The focal point for many people is food. It can be simply snacks and drinks, although the usual main event is a family dinner where people gather and feast together on classic Mexican dishes and the favorite food of the deceased. Some will lay out a plate of food at dinner for every honored soul. The food and drink for the meals and the *ofrendas* are believed to have their "essence" eaten by the returned spirits.

Below: *Mariachi band at a Day of the Dead festival, San Miguel de Allende, Guanajuato, Mexico, 2016.*

DIRECTORY OF FESTIVALS

Most families celebrate the Day of the Dead privately, but there are public displays in the entrances of museums and galleries in Mexico that you can visit to experience the festivities. Nearly all cities and towns have a public square, called a *zócalo*, with music and events, and they are happy to have (respectful) visitors. Most places around the world with large communities of Mexicans will have public Day of the Dead celebrations to bring the community together.

Celebrations vary throughout Mexico. The bigger, bolder festivities are full of color in the states of Michoacan, Chiapas, and Mexico City.

MEXICO
Oaxaca
Oaxaca in particular is famous for loud, exuberant public processions and sand tapestries.

Mexico City
The Day of the Dead street parade is a modern creation. It came about after the opening scene of the Bond film *Spectre* (2015) brought Day of the Dead to popular consciousness abroad. Now, to meet public expectations, a parade of a thousand costumed dancers and actors takes place once a year on a day leading up to the actual Day of the Dead.

It is full of skeletons, La Catrinas, marigolds, music, and color. The *zócalo* is the large focal point of public celebrations. The large space is filled with altars and visitors.

Aguascalientes
The creator of the image of La Catrina, José Guadalupe Posada, was born here. So every year from October 28 to November 2 the Festival de las Calaveras (Festival of Skulls) celebrates the engraver's creations. Arts and crafts are on display alongside a festival of food, music, and theater in the city. It culminates with a parade of *calaveras*.

Riviera Maya
For a glitzy, theme-park version of the Day of the Dead, the Riviera Maya holds a Festival de la Vida y la Muerte (Festival of Life and Death) every year from October 30 to November 2.

Chiapa de Corzo
A visit to this town in Chiapas is a chance to see a cemetery decorated for the Day of the Dead. There is ample color, music, and cheer throughout the night, and visitors can (respectfully) visit.

Left: *Day of the Dead festival, Oaxaca, Mexico, 2014.*
Below: *Musicians playing in front of a columbarium during Day of the Dead celebrations in Morelia, Mexico, 2014.*

U.S.

Chicago

The city holds one of the longest running celebrations of the Day of the Dead outside of Mexico. There are altar exhibitions in conjunction with the National Museum of Mexican Art, along with other art and mixed-media installations on the exterior of the museum. It is all in celebration and recognition of the large Mexican community in the windy city.

Los Angeles

Olvera Street in the historic downtown Mexican marketplace holds a week-long festival finishing on November 2. The festivities include altar displays, street performances and dance, candlelight processions, and craft workshops for children and adults.

Albuquerque

The Muertos y Marigolds Parade and Celebration in South Valley is a popular event to mark the Day of the Dead by decorating cars and people with the brightly colored flowers.

Fort Lauderdale

A large street festival on November 2 in south Florida culminates with a parade of thousands of skeletons. Mariachis and folklore performances add to the celebrations.

TEMPLATES

PAGES 18-19   CANDLE HOLDERS

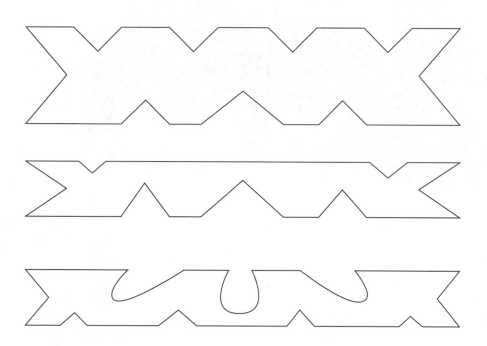

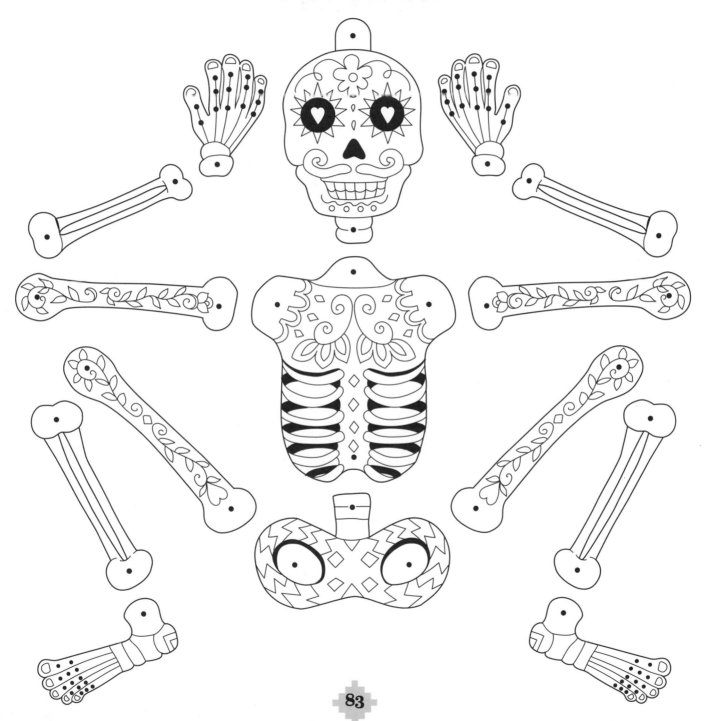

83

Cut along here
for the insert

Cut this way for
the invite to stand
up properly

Cut this way for the
back to be identical
to the front

CURRENTLY 75%

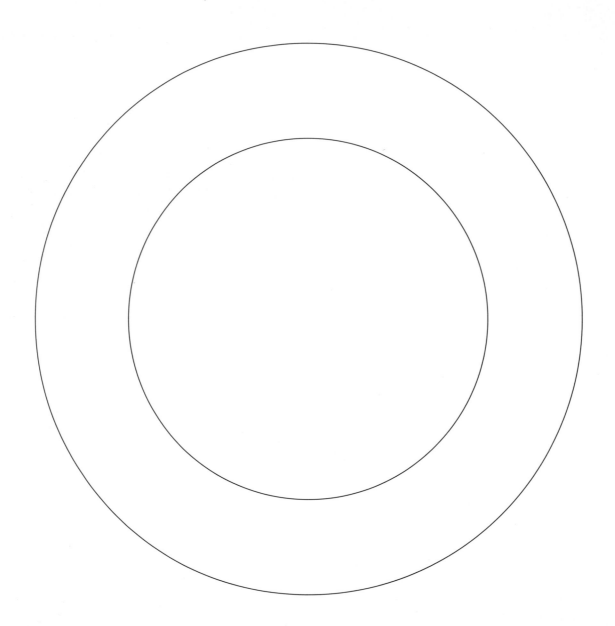

RESIZE TO 200%

Ranunculus

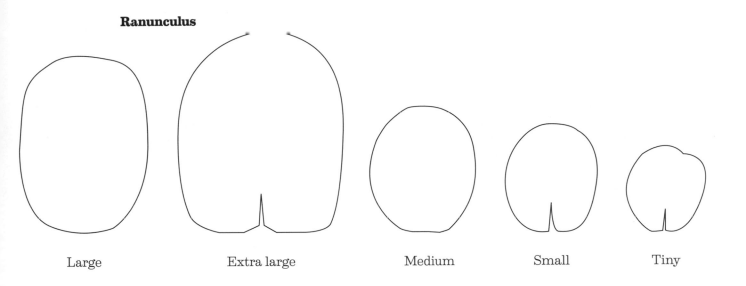

Large   Extra large   Medium   Small   Tiny

Leaves

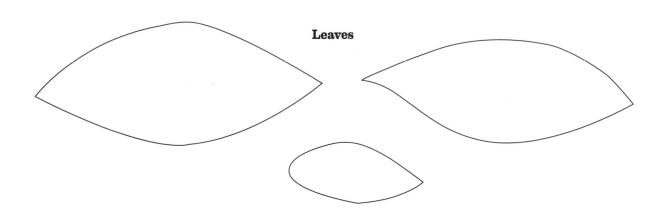

Tab — — — — — — — — — —

INDEX

CREDITS

THE CONTRIBUTORS

Paula Pascual is a Spanish designer, paper crafter, and blogger. She has worked in the UK paper craft industry for the last 14 years. Her work has appeared in *Crafts Beautiful* and *Cardmaking and Papercraft* magazines. She has authored three books, including *Paper Pom-Poms* (Carlton Books). She has designed product collections for companies such as Sizzix, and is currently a creative demonstrator for Tonic Studios.

Phillip Tang is a travel writer for guidebooks and online, covering Asian and Latin American countries, including Mexico, where he lived for three years.

Rebecca Woods was a cookbook editor for years before retraining as a chef. She is now a food stylist and recipe developer for books and magazine publishers, as well as an editorial consultant on cookbooks. She lives in London.